ISBN: 978-87-85240-12-5

PUBLISHED BY
AURORA INTERNATIONAL PUBLISHING

Tranquil Earth Alliance's Comprehensive Parole Release Plan Packet

By DeAngelo Capone

Executive Summary

Parole Release Plan Overview

Name of Individual:
Inmate or DOC Number:
Current Facility:
Parole Eligibility Date:
Proposed Release Date or Window:
Proposed Release Location (City, State):
Supervising Authority After Release:

Purpose of This Plan

This Executive Summary provides a concise overview of the attached Comprehensive Parole Release Plan Packet. The purpose is to present a clear, verifiable, and realistic release plan that addresses risk management, stability, and accountability, and demonstrates readiness for parole and community supervision.

Housing Plan

Approved residence address:
Type of housing (family, sponsor, transitional, independent):
Primary household contact:
Housing rules and restrictions acknowledged:
☐Yes ☐No
Backup housing plan in place: ☐Yes ☐No

Summary statement:
Briefly describe why this housing is stable, lawful, and appropriate, and how it reduces risk.

Income and Employment Plan

Primary income source upon release:
Employer or income pathway:
Start date or interim plan:
Transportation to work or appointments:

Summary statement:
Briefly explain how lawful income will be maintained and how employment or benefits support stability.

Treatment and Health Continuity

Medical care provider identified: ☐Yes ☐No
Mental health services arranged if applicable: Yes / No
Substance use treatment or recovery supports arranged if applicable: ☐Yes ☐No

Summary statement:
Briefly describe continuity of care, appointments scheduled, and compliance plan.

Daily Structure and Supervision Readiness

Reporting plan understood and accepted: ☐Yes ☐No
Daily schedule prepared: ☐Yes ☐No
Transportation plan for reporting and services: ☐Yes ☐No

Summary statement:
Briefly describe daily structure, reporting readiness, and ability to comply with supervision requirements.

Risk Management and Accountability

Primary identified risks:
Key prevention strategies:
Contingency plans in place: ☐Yes ☐No

Summary statement:
Briefly explain how risks are recognized, managed, and monitored, including early warning signs and response steps.

Verification and Support

Third party verification included for housing: ☐Yes ☐No
Employment or income verification included if available: ☐Yes ☐No
Sponsor or support letters included: ☐Yes ☐No

Summary statement:
Briefly describe the support network and verification provided.

Closing Statement

This plan does not claim perfection. It demonstrates preparedness, accountability, and a structured pathway for lawful and stable reintegration under supervision. All major claims are supported by documentation contained in this packet.

Introduction

Tranquil Earth Alliance's Comprehensive Parole Release Plan Packet was developed as a result of more than three decades of experiences within correctional institutions and direct observation of the parole process, along with shared testimonies of parole hearings, supervision outcomes, and reentry barriers faced by incarcerated people across multiple states and international correctional systems.

I have repeatedly witnessed and been given accounts of common and preventable failures in the parole process, including individuals appealing hearings without structured or verifiable plans, limited help from institutional staff, and recidivism driven by inadequate or untimely preparation and unrealistic planning. Many individuals have been released with vague housing arrangements, unstable income plans, or no continuity of care, despite genuine efforts to successfully return to society.

This packet was created in response to those gaps. Its purpose is to provide a practical and structured plan that incarcerated people can use to prepare for parole and conditional release, regardless of incarceration state.

The format intentionally avoids reliance on informal practices so that the packet can function across states, and, where applicable, across national penal systems.

The structure and contents of this packet are informed by widely accepted reentry principles and evidence-informed supervision practices. These principles have been collected from a variety of professional, correctional practices, community-based sources, program models, reentry organizations, and the lived experience of individuals navigating release and supervision. No single institution or state defines the approach used here.

While my broader work is driven by Wiccan ethics that promote responsibility, truthfulness, harm reduction, and accountability, this packet itself is not a religious document. It does not promote or require any belief system or spiritual practice. All guidance contained in this packet is intended to support public safety, lawful behavior, and successful reintegration.

This packet can be used by incarcerated individuals, their support networks, reentry organizations, and supervision stakeholders as a shared planning tool. Its goal is not to guarantee release, but to improve verifiable release readiness at the point of parole decision-making.

Rehabilitative Progress

This section intends to explain personal growth, behavioral change, and rehabilitative work. Parole Boards look for evidence that the person appearing before them has developed insight into past thinking and actions, taken responsibility for harm caused, developed the skills needed to live a crime-free life and function responsibly in society.

This section should focus on demonstrated change. The goal is to show how the person's thinking, decision making, and lifestyle choices have improved through reflection, programming, education, and pro-social behavior.

Understanding the Causes of the Offense

The person should briefly describe the factors that contributed to the offense. This is not a moment for legal arguments or to minimize responsibility. It is an explanation that shows insight into past decision making and circumstances.

Examples of contributing factors may include substance abuse, gang involvement, poor problem-solving skills, untreated or misdiagnosed mental health issues, impulsiveness, or other personal or environmental pressures.

The focus should be on demonstrating an understanding of these factors and how they led to harmful decisions.

Remorse and Accepting Responsibility

Parole Boards look for clear acceptance of responsibility for the offense. This means acknowledging the harm done to victims, family, and the community.

Remorse should be expressed sincerely and without shifting blame to others or circumstances. The person may describe how their understanding of the offense has changed over time and what they have learned about the impact of their actions.

Remorse is most meaningful when the person can pair it with concrete behavioral change.

Personal Accountability

This explains how the person has changed their thinking patterns and decision-making processes, such as building coping skills, recognizing negative influences, or using better judgment in difficult situations.

The person may describe tools or strategies learned through programming, counseling, or spiritual work that help guide their day-to-day decision making.

Examples of cognitive change may include:

- Taking personal responsibility for choices
- Improved impulse control and emotional regulation
- Developing empathy and regard toward others
- Learning conflict resolution and communication skills
- Rejecting criminal thinking patterns or harmful peer influences

Pro-Social Attitudes and Behavior

Parole Boards look for evidence that a person has adopted constructive attitudes and behaviors that meet societal norms.

This may include mentoring others, participating in peer support programs, receiving consistently positive work evaluations, involvement in faith-based programs, or contributing to community service.

Evidence of Rehabilitation

In addition to describing personal change, this section should reference evidence of progress.

Educational achievements such as GED completion, college courses, or vocational certificates.

Completion of treatment programs such as substance abuse programs, cognitive behavioral programs, or anger management.

Participation in counseling, therapy, or recovery support programs.

Demonstrating reliability and responsibility.

Positive institutional conduct and reduced disciplinary issues.

Supporting documentation such as certificates, transcripts, or program completion records should be included later in the verification section of the packet.

Connection to the Release Plan

The final part of this section should briefly explain how the lessons learned during incarceration connect to the individual's release plan.

For example, someone who addressed substance abuse issues may describe how they will continue recovery through community treatment or support groups. Someone who improved emotional regulation may explain how they will manage stress through structured routines and positive community support. This helps the Parole Board see that rehabilitation will continue after release.

Progress Since Last Review

This section documents measurable progress made since the individual's last Parole Board hearing. It is intended to provide the Parole Board with a clear update on continued rehabilitation and improved behavior.

Parole Boards evaluate progress over time.

Demonstrating continued effort and improvement between hearings can strengthen the overall release plan and show commitment to long-term change.

Timeframe Covered

Date of last Parole Board hearing or review: __________

Time period covered in this update: __________

Summary of Progress

Provide a brief overview of the most important changes since the last review. Focus on improvements in behavior and participation in programming completed since the last review.

Examples may include:

- Sustained positive conduct
- Completion of additional programs
- Development of new skills
- Strengthening of release plan components

Institutional Conduct Since Last Review

Describe conduct during the period since the last hearing.

Include:

- Any disciplinary infractions and explanation if applicable
- Length of time without infractions
- Changes in behavior or decision making

The focus should be on demonstrating improved stability, accountability, and consistency.

Program and Educational Progress

List any programs, courses, or training completed since the last review.

Include:

- Program name
- Completion date
- Skills or knowledge gained

Explain how these programs contributed to personal development and preparation for release.

Work Assignments and Performance

Describe any work assignments held since the last review.

Include:

- Type of work
- Length of time in the position
- Any positive evaluations or increased responsibilities

Highlight improvements in work ethic, responsibility, and reliability.

Updated Release Plan Elements

Identify any improvements made to the release plan since the last review.

Examples may include:

- Securing or improving housing arrangements
- Establishing employment opportunities or pathways
- Confirming treatment providers or appointments
- Strengthening community support

Explain how these updates improve stability and readiness for release.

Completion of additional programming

If the Parole Board provided recommendations or concerns during the last review, explain how those have been addressed.

Examples may include:

- Completion of additional programming
- Improved conduct
- Strengthened release plan components

Demonstrating responsiveness to the Parole Board's feedback shows accountability and commitment to improvement.

Commitment to Continued Progress

Conclude this section by reaffirming commitment to continued personal development and successful reintegration.

This section should clearly show that progress is ongoing and that the individual has remained focused on improvement regardless of past outcomes.

Institutional Conduct, Rule Infractions, and Program Participation

Parole Boards review a person's institutional conduct to understand how the person has behaved while incarcerated. Conduct reports, program participation, work assignments, and educational accomplishments help the Parole Board evaluate readiness for release.

While the Parole Board will have access to institutional records, individuals may be asked to explain past rule infractions or describe their participation in programs and work assignments. This section allows the individual to provide context.

Institutional Conduct and Behavior

The individual should summarize their overall conduct during incarceration. This may include years of disciplinary-free behavior, positive evaluations from staff, consistent work performance, or participation in programs.

The goal is not to claim perfection but to show patterns of responsible behavior, compliance with institutional rules, and commitment to personal improvement.

If the individual has maintained a strong conduct record, they should briefly explain how they have focused on maintaining discipline and avoiding conflicts.

Explaining Rule Infractions

For the majority of incarcerated persons, rule infractions have occurred. Rule infractions should be addressed honestly and directly.

When discussing an infraction, the individual should briefly explain:

- The nature of the violation
- The circumstances surrounding the incident
- What they learned from the experience
- What steps they took to prevent similar behavior in the future

The focus should remain on personal responsibility and the lessons gained rather than deflecting blame toward staff, other incarcerated persons, or institutional conditions.

Demonstrating Behavioral Change

If earlier misconduct occurred during the first years of incarceration, the individual may explain how their behavior has changed over time. For example, a person may describe how early disciplinary issues occurred before participating in treatment programs or before developing better coping strategies.

Showing improvement over time can be more important to Parole Boards than having a perfect record.

Education and Program Participation

Most institutions can provide documentation showing educational achievements, vocational training, and program completion. Individuals should list these accomplishments clearly so they can be verified by institutional records.

Examples may include:

- GED completion or high school diploma
- College courses or correspondence education
- Vocational or technical training programs
- Victim awareness programs
- Substance abuse treatment programs
- Cognitive behavioral programs
- Reentry programs
- Anger management or emotional regulation programs
- Life skills or job readiness training

Each program should be listed with the approximate completion date and the institution where it was completed.

Institutional Work Assignments

Work assignments are another indicator of responsibility and reliability. Individuals may describe the jobs they have held while incarcerated, including the length of time in the position and the duties performed.

Examples may include maintenance, food service, sanitation, program aide work, tutoring, or other institutional employment.

If available, positive work evaluations from supervisors may be included in the verification section of the packet.

Supporting Documentation

Whenever possible, documentation should be attached to support the information listed in this section. This may include certificates, transcripts, program participation records, or work evaluation reports.

These documents allow Parole Boards to verify accomplishments quickly and reinforce the credibility of the information presented.

Connection to Rehabilitation

The final portion of this section should briefly explain how institutional programs, work assignments, and improved conduct contributed to personal development.

For example, a person may explain how participation in a substance abuse program helped them understand addiction triggers, or how work assignments helped develop responsibility, time management, and teamwork skills.

This helps demonstrate that institutional experiences contributed to the individual's rehabilitation and preparation for successful reintegration.

How Parole Boards and Supervision Agencies Evaluate Release Plans

Parole Boards and Supervision Agencies typically evaluate parole release plans to help determine suitability for parole using three core questions: Risk, Stability, and Accountability.

Risk asks:

What is the likelihood of criminal behavior or supervision violations, and what specific factors increase or reduce that risk. They will look for a plan that identifies risk triggers and shows concrete controls such as a structured schedule, stable housing, legal income, treatment compliance, positive social support, and clear avoidance of high-risk people, places, and things.

Stability asks:

Can this person live day to day without returning to instability. They will look for housing that is lawful, safe, and suitable, realistic income goals, a routine that reduces idle time, access to medical and behavioral health care, and a plan for basics like IDs, finances, and communication.

Accountability asks:

Will this person follow the law and conditions of supervision, report as required and respond appropriately to direction and correction. Decision makers look for insight into past behaviors, evidence of change, and a track record of program participation, skills gained from that programming, and positive institutional conduct. They also weigh third party verification from staff, counselors, educators, employers, mentors, and others who can speak to day-to-day reliability and reintegration readiness.

A strong parole plan packet does not try to prove the incarcerated person is perfect. It makes it easier for decision makers to say "yes" because the plan shows manageable risk and strong controls, and because an individual's claims can be verified quickly.

What This Parole Plan Packet Does:

- Organize the release plan into a consistent format that Parole Boards and Supervision Agencies can review clearly.
- Provide space for documents: letters, confirmations, program certificates, employment contacts if ready, treatment plan, and transportation arrangements.
- Translate goals into commitments, timelines, and contingency plans so the Parole plan is not simply a promise.
- Reduce reasons which may give cause for denial such as vague housing, loose work plans, absence of continued treatment, etc.

What This Packet Does Not Do:

- Guarantee parole or any specific decision.
- Replace legal advice or strategy.
- Override statutory restrictions, victim related restrictions, or mandatory conditions.
- Excuse dishonesty, omissions, or inflated claims. Those typically backfire.

Important Notes on Honesty, Verification, and Accountability

Honesty is not a moral add-on. It is risk control. Parole Boards and Supervising Agencies treat falsehoods and surprises as major risk indicators. Do not hide relevant facts that will surface anyway, such as substance use history, reasons for prior supervision failures, or conflict history. Address them with a concrete and authentic management plan.

Verification is what turns a claim into a functional reality. Any statement that matters should be reinforced by a document or a contact who will confirm it. Examples could be housing letters that name the address and rules, employer letters that confirm employment starting dates, and sponsor letters clearly stating what they will and will not do.

Accountability means naming responsibilities and measuring follow through. The plan should describe who is responsible for each step, the expected date of completion, and what proof will be provided. If something changes, the plan must be updated, not defended.

Avoid these common missteps:

- Vague housing: "I can live with family" without an address, rules, or written confirmation.
- Vague income: "I will find work" without a pathway, contacts, or a temporary plan.
- No treatment continuity: "I will go to counseling" without an appointment or provider plan.
- Over-promising: support-people making guarantees they cannot sustain.
- Copy-pasted language: generic plans that do not match the person's actual history, risks, and restrictions.

Step by Step Guide to Use This Packet

Step 1: Identify the target decision.

Define the hearing, the expected date range, and the supervising authority after release. Prepare the plan so it is workable for both the Parole Board and the Supervising Agency.

Step 2: Confirm the foundation.

Secure housing, identification, and a reliable contact method. Confirm transportation and lawful income pathway, including temporary options if employment is not immediately available.

Step 3: Complete the core plan sections.

Document treatment continuity (medical, mental health, and substance use if applicable), community support, daily schedule, and financial responsibilities.

Step 4: Add verification documents.

Attach letters and confirmations that support each claim. Every major claim should be backed by third party verification when possible.

Step 5: Add risk management and contingency plans.

Identify key risks and early warning signs, then document prevention steps and backup plans for housing disruption, employment changes, relapse risk, transportation failure, or loss of support.

Step 6: Align to likely supervision conditions.

Complete the conditions acknowledgment page and explain how each condition will be met. Do not argue the conditions in the plan. Demonstrate compliance capability.

Step 7: Quality control review.

Check internal consistency: names, phone numbers, addresses, dates, and schedules. Remove anything that cannot be verified. Use language that clearly supports each claim.

Step 8: Produce the final packet.

Print or assemble in a clear order a table of contents, tabs, or section headers, and a one-page summary for quick review. Keep copies for the Parole authority, Supervising Agency, and the sponsor.

How State-Specific Supplements Work

The main parole plan packet stays the same across states. The supplement is a short add-on that adapts the packet to a particular state's rules and expectations. The supplement typically includes:

- State terminology and agency names used in that jurisdiction.
- Common required forms, release plan templates, and risk assessment references where known.
- Housing eligibility rules and restrictions relevant to that state or county.
- Supervision conditions that are frequently imposed in that jurisdiction and how to document compliance.
- Local provider directories or referral pathways if Tranquil Earth Alliance maintains them.
- Any state-specific documentation standards, such as notarization preferences or verification formats.

Once the packet is completed, then the supplement is attached for the relevant state. If a person has the option and may parole to more than one state, produce a single packet and two alternate supplements, one per destination.

Identification and Release Information

This section establishes the individual's identity, confirms release details, and provides reliable contact information for post-release supervision. All information in this section must be accurate, current and verifiable.

Personal Identification

Legal Name (as listed with DOC):

Date of Birth:

DOC number:

Current facility and housing unit:

State-issued ID or driver's license secured: ☐Yes ☐No

If No, do you plan to obtain ID documented: ☐Yes ☐No

If ID is not currently held, specify:

- Type of ID to be obtained
- Issuing ID
- Appointment date or application plan
- Temporary identification or verification available upon release

Release Details

Type of release being requested or anticipated:

Parole eligibility date:

Projected release date or window:

Releasing authority:

Conditions affecting release timing, if any:

Examples include detainers, program completion requirements, interstate transfer approval, or administrative holds.

Proposed Release Destination

Proposed release address (street, city, state, ZIP):

County of release:

State of release:

Is this address different from sentencing jurisdiction?

☐Yes ☐No:

If yes, interstate compact or transfer required:

☐Yes ☐No

If required, status of transfer request or plan:

Primary Contact Information Upon Release

Primary phone number to be used after release:

Secondary or backup phone number:

Email address if available:

Transportation from Facility

Transportation arranged for day of release: Yes / No

Method of transportation:

Name of person or service providing transportation:

Destination upon release:

If transportation is not confirmed, describe the interim plan and timeline to secure it.

Supervision Intake Readiness

Supervising Agency expected upon release:

Office location if known:

Reporting timeframe expected (for example, same day, 24 hours, 72 hours):

Plan to report as required:

Describe how transportation, documentation, and contact will be managed to ensure timely reporting.

Verification Attached for This Section

Check all that apply and attach documentation where available:

- Copy of identification or receipt for ID application
- Release paperwork or eligibility notice
- Address verification
- Transportation confirmation
- Contact person confirmation

Housing Plan

This section documents where the individual will live upon release and demonstrates that the residence is lawful, stable, and suitable for supervision. Housing is a primary factor in parole decisions and must be specific, verified, and realistic.

Primary Housing Information

Proposed residence address (street, city, state, ZIP):

County and State of residence:

Type of housing:

Family, sponsor, transitional, independent, or program-based

Name of primary housing contact:

Relationship to individual:

Length of time individual may reside at this address:

Household Composition

List all adults residing at the address:

List any minors residing at the address:

Note any individuals with criminal justice involvement if applicable:

Housing Rules and Expectations

Curfew or house rules:

Substance use restrictions:

Visitor restrictions:

Other relevant household expectations:

Acknowledgment that all household rules will be followed: ☐Yes ☐No

Supervision Compatibility

Is the residence compatible with supervision conditions: ☐Yes ☐No

If restrictions apply, describe how compliance will be maintained:

Examples include distance restrictions, electronic monitoring, search conditions, or victim-related restrictions.

Stability Assessment

Brief narrative explaining why this housing is stable and appropriate. Address duration, structure, supervision compatibility, and how the environment supports lawful behavior and reintegration.

Backup Housing Plan

Backup residence address if primary housing becomes unavailable:

Contact person for backup housing:

Conditions or limitations of backup housing:

Verification Attached

Attach written housing verification that includes:

- Full address
- Name and contact information of household contact
- Duration and conditions of residence
- Acknowledgment of supervision and house rules.

Income and Employment Plan

This section documents how lawful income will be obtained and maintained upon release. The plan may include employment, benefits, stipends, or other lawful support, and must demonstrate financial stability and reduced risk of recidivism.

Primary Income Source

Primary source of income upon release:

Employer, agency, or support source:

Position or type of work if applicable:

Start date or expected timeline:

Hours per week:

Estimated income:

Employment Pathway if Not Yet Secured

Describe active job search plan, vocational pathway, or transitional employment program. Include realistic steps, contacts, and timelines.

Benefits or Interim Support

Public benefits applied for or eligible for:

Application status or appointment date:

Temporary financial support if applicable:

Transportation to Income Source

Primary transportation method:

Distance to work or appointments:

Backup transportation plan:

Stability Narrative

Brief explanation of how lawful income will be maintained and how this plan supports financial responsibility and compliance with supervision obligations.

Verification Attached

Attach documents where available, such as:

- Employment offers or employer letters
- Job search or program enrollment confirmation
- Benefits application or eligibility documentation

Treatment and Health Continuity

This section demonstrates continuity of medical, mental health, and substance use treatment when applicable.

Medical Care

Primary medical provider identified: ☐Yes ☐No

Provider name and location:

Mental Health Care if Applicable

Mental health provider identified: ☐Yes ☐No

Type of services: counseling, psychiatry, therapy

Appointment scheduled or plan in place: ☐Yes ☐No

Substance Use Treatment or Recovery Support if Applicable

Treatment or recovery program identified: Yes / No

Type of program or support: recovery group, outpatient treatment, sponsor, medication-assisted treatment

Appointment or meeting plan in place: ☐Yes ☐No

Medication Continuity

Prescribed medications documented: ☐Yes ☐No

Plan to continue medications without interruption:

☐Yes ☐No

Stability Narrative

Briefly explain how treatment continuity supports stability, compliance, and risk reduction.

Verification Attached

Attach documentation, such as:

- Appointment confirmations
- Provider letters
- Program enrollment confirmations

Daily schedule and Community Structure

This section demonstrates how time will be structured to reduce idle time and support accountability, pro-social engagement, and compliance with supervision.

Daily and Weekly Schedule

Outline a realistic weekday and weekend schedule, including:

- Work and job search activities
- Treatment or appointments
- Reporting requirements
- Household responsibilities
- Rest and self-care

Community and Pro-Social Supports

List community supports that promote accountability and reintegration, such as:

- Family or mentor support
- Faith or spiritual community
- Faith group, mentoring, or other pro-social engagement
- Peer recovery support
- Educational or vocational programs

Structure Narrative

Briefly explain how this schedule and community structure reduce risk and support lawful behavior.

Support Letters and Community Support Documentation

Support letters provide the Parole Board with confirmation that positive relationships and community support is available after release. These letters help demonstrate that the individual will not be returning to isolation or an unstable environment.

Support letters should come from people who know the individual, understand their plans, and are willing to assist in their successful reintegration into society.

Possible Sources of Support Letters

Support letters may come from a variety of people or organizations involved in the individual's life.

Examples of Support Persons:

- Family members
- Mentors
- Faith Leaders or spiritual advisors
- Community organizations
- Recovery sponsors or support group leaders
- Employers or potential employers
- Reentry programs or service providers

The most effective letters are written by people who have direct knowledge of the individual's character, growth, and release readiness.

Information Support Letters Should Include

Support letters should be clear, honest, and specific. Each letter should include:

- The writer's full name and contact information
- Their relationship to the individual
- How long they have known the individual
- Observations about the individual's growth or character
- A statement of support for the individual's release
- A description of any assistance they are willing to provide.

Examples of Assistance:

- Housing
- Employment Opportunities
- Transportation
- Mentoring
- Recovery Support

General Guidelines for Support Letters

Support letters should focus on the individual's habilitation and reentry readiness. Writers should avoid minimizing the offense or criticizing the justice system.

Template for a Support Letter

Date:

To the Parole Board,

My name is [Name]. I am writing in support of [Individual's Name] as they come before you for consideration of release.

I have known [Individual's Name] for [length of time] and know them through [their relationship such as faith leader, mentor, employer, or otherwise].

During the time I have known them, I have observed significant personal growth and positive change in their thinking and behavior. I believe they have worked hard to take responsibility for their past actions and prepare themselves for a productive life after release.

If they are granted parole, I am willing to support their successful reintegration. This support may include [describe specific assistance such as housing, recovery support, transportation, employment, mentoring].

I believe [Individual's Name] is committed to living responsibly and contributing positively to the community. I respectfully ask the Parole Board to consider their progress and preparation for release.

Sincerely,

Name
Address
Email
Phone Number

Submitting Support Letters

Support letters may be included in the parole packet and attached to the verification and supporting documentation section.

In some states, letters may also be submitted directly to the Parole Board in advance of the hearing. Verify submission procedures with the relevant parole authority to ensure letters are received and properly added to case file.

Information for Families and Supporters

Family members, friends, and community supporters play a critical role in successful reentry. This section provides guidance on how supporters can assist in a way that promotes stability, accountability, and compliance with supervision.

Parole Boards not only evaluate the individual, but also the environment the individual will return to. Clear, realistic support improves credibility and reduces perceived risk.

Understanding the Role of Support

Support does not mean removing responsibility from the individual. Effective support reinforces structure, accountability, and lawful behavior.

Supporters should understand that the individual will be required to follow supervision conditions, maintain schedules, attend appointments, and comply with all legal requirements.

The role of the supporter is to assist, not to replace responsibility.

Preparing the Home Environment

If the individual is returning to a family or sponsor residence, the home environment should be stable and compatible with supervision.

Supporters should be prepared to:

- Maintain a safe and lawful environment (no weapons, such as firearms, paintball guns, etc. or drugs)
- Support curfew or supervision restrictions
- Limit exposure to negative influences
- Encourage compliance with treatment and reporting requirements

Household expectations should be clear before release and consistently enforced after release

Setting Clear Expectations and Boundaries

Supporters should establish clear expectations regarding behavior, responsibilities, and household rules.

Examples include:

- Curfew expectations
- Substance use restrictions
- No Contact Orders (if any)
- Participation in work or treatment
- Respect for household rules

Avoiding Overpromising

Supporters should only commit to what they can realistically provide. Overpromising can create instability and may negatively impact parole decisions if plans fall apart.

Support should be specific, realistic, and sustainable.

Examples of appropriate support:

- Provide stable housing
- Providing spiritual care or recovery support
- Offering transportation to work or appointments
- Assisting with job searches or connections
- Providing emotional support and encouragement

Supporters should avoid making guarantees they cannot maintain.

Communication with the Individual

Open and consistent communication is important. Supporters should encourage honesty, accountability, and problem-solving.

If challenges arise, supporters should guide the individual toward appropriate solutions such as contacting their supervising parole officer, attending scheduled appointments, or accessing available resources.

Responding to Challenges

Reentry may involve stress, setbacks, or unexpected challenges. Supporters should be prepared to respond in a way that promotes stability.

This may include:

- Encouraging the individual to follow their contingency plan
- Supporting continued participation in treatment or recovery programs.
- Maintaining structure and routine
- Avoid escalation of conflict

Supporters should reinforce the importance of always staying compliant with supervision requirements.

Coordination with Supervision and Services

Supporters should understand that Supervision Agencies and service providers play a central role in the individual's reentry.

When appropriate, supporters may:

- Assist with transportation to supervision appointments
- Help maintain schedules and reminders
- Encourage compliance with all parole guidelines or supervision directives

All communication with supervising agencies should respect boundaries and follow legal requirements.

Risk Management and Contingency Planning

This section identifies known risk factors and documents specific strategies to prevent parole violations or reoffending. It also demonstrates preparedness to cope healthily with challenges when they arise. Parole Boards rely heavily on the information provided in this section to assess realism and accountability.

Identified Risk Factors

List the primary risks. Examples may include but are not limited to:

- Substance use relapse risk
- Association with high-risk people
- Unstable employment history
- Unaddressed mental health symptoms
- Transportation barriers
- Prior supervision failures

Each risk listed should be specific to the history and circumstances of the individual.

Early Warning Signs

For each identified risk, list observable early warning signs that indicate increased risk. Examples include abrupt changes in routine, missed appointments, social withdrawal, increased stress, or contact with prohibited individuals.

Prevention Strategies

Describe the concrete steps in place to reduce risk, such as:

- Structured daily schedule
- Treatment or recovery engagement
- Accountability check-ins with sponsors or mentors
- Avoidance plans for people, places, and situations
- Use of coping skills or relapse prevention tools

Contingency Plans

Describe the response plan if a risk escalates or a plan component fails. Address scenarios such as:

- Housing disruption
- Loss of employment or income
- Increased substance use risk
- Mental health crisis
- Transportation failure

Each contingency should include who will be notified, what immediate steps will be taken, and how compliance with supervision will be maintained.

Risk Management Summary

Briefly summarize how risks are recognized, monitored, and managed in a way that supports public safety, compliance, and successful reintegration.

Continuity Plan if Parole Is Denied

Parole Boards make decisions based on many factors, and approval for release is not guaranteed. This section helps the individual demonstrate a commitment to continued release preparation even if parole is not granted at the current hearing.

Parole Boards look for signs of persistence and maturity. Showing a plan for continued progress indicates a focus on long-term change rather than only the immediate outcome of the hearing.

Continued Personal Development

If parole is denied, the individual should continue focusing on personal development and rehabilitation by pursuing other opportunities that support growth and stability.

The individual may describe areas where they intend to improve, such as strengthening coping skills, developing additional job training, or completing additional programming.

Parole Board Feedback

If the Parole Board offers feedback after a denial, their feedback should be taken seriously and addressed directly.

Examples may include:

- Completing additional programming
- Maintaining a longer period of positive conduct
- Participating in counseling or treatment
- Strengthening the release plan

The individual should document how they plan to address these areas of concern and provide proof of completion before the next hearing.

Maintaining Positive Institutional Conduct

Maintaining positive conduct remains essential after a parole denial to demonstrate stability and commitment to change.

Mental and Emotional Resilience

A parole denial can be discouraging. The individual may describe healthy ways they plan to manage frustration or discouragement and avoid falling into a "nothing I do will matter" mindset, such as seeking support from counselors, mental health services, participating in peer support groups, engaging in faith or spiritual practices, or maintaining a healthy routine.

This shows the Parole Board that the individual has developed the emotional tools necessary to respond constructively to setbacks.

Updating the Release Plan

If parole is denied, the individual should continue strengthening their release plan.

This may include updating housing arrangements, maintaining contact with potential employers, maintaining community support relationships, or expanding treatment plans.

Keeping the release plan current ensures that the individual will be better prepared for the next parole review.

Supervision Conditions Acknowledgment

This section demonstrates understanding of and readiness to comply with supervision conditions. It does not challenge conditions. It explains how they will be achieved.

Anticipated Supervision Conditions

List common or anticipated conditions such as:

- Reporting requirements
- Drug or alcohol testing
- Curfew or movement restrictions
- Employment or programming requirements
- Search conditions
- No-contact or geographic restrictions

Compliance Plan

For each anticipated condition, briefly explain how compliance will be achieved. Examples include transportation arrangements for reporting, treatment tracking, or housing compatibility with monitoring requirements.

Fees and Financial Obligations

List anticipated supervision fees, court costs, restitution, or other obligations.

Describe how these obligations will be managed within the income plan.

Supervision Readiness Statement

Brief statement affirming understanding of supervision authority, willingness to comply with directives, and commitment to maintaining open communication with supervising officers.

Verification and Supporting Documentation

This section consolidates all documents that verify the claims made throughout the packet. Clear organization here reduces review time and increases credibility.

Document Index

Attach and label documents under the following categories as applicable:

- Identification documents or application receipts
- Housing verification letters
- Employment offers or job pathway documentation
- Benefits or financial support documentation
- Treatment provider confirmations
- Sponsor and support letters
- Program certificates and institutional records

Document Standards

All documents should include current contact information, be legible, and reflect current plans. Outdated or conflicting documents should be removed.

Final Attestation and Submission

This section affirms the accuracy and completeness of the packet at the time of submission.

Attestation Statement

I affirm that the information contained in this Comprehensive Parole Release Plan Packet is accurate to the best of my knowledge and reflects my current and intended release plan. I understand that providing false or misleading information may negatively impact parole decisions and supervision.

Signature of Individual:

Printed Name:

Date:

Optional Attestation

Sponsor, Case Manager, or Support Person

Name and Role:
Signature:
Date:

Packet Submission Notes

Date of Submission:
Submitted to:
Copies provided to:

State-Specific Supplement

State:
Parole Authority:
Supervision Agency:
Report Requirements:

Housing Restrictions

Zoning restrictions:
Prohibited counties or exclusion zones:
Residency approval process:
Co-resident background checks:

Required Forms and Documentation

Official release plan:
Interstate Compact documentation:
Specific housing verification:
Other state-required disclosures:

Unique Compliance Considerations

Drug testing frequency and method:
Curfew enforcement:
Electronic monitoring practices:
Travel approval procedures:
Fees and payment structure:

Local Resources

Reentry resource directories:
State workforce programs:
Medicaid enrollment process:
Housing assistance portals:

State-Specific Supplement Example

State: North Carolina

Parole Authority: North Carolina Post-Release Supervision and Parole Commission

Supervision Agency: North Carolina Department of Adult Correction, Division of Community Supervision

North Carolina's criminal justice system operates under structured sentencing for most criminal offences, with parole primarily applicable to pre-structured sentencing cases and specific categories. Post-release supervision is mandatory for certain criminal offenses.

Report Requirements

Reporting Timeframe: Parolees are typically required to report to their assigned supervising officer as directed in release instructions.

Ongoing Reporting: Reporting frequency varies by supervision level but commonly includes in-person meetings at least monthly during early supervision, with possible changes based on risk level.

Special intake requirements: Orientation sessions may be required that include a review of parole conditions, drug testing procedures, and fee assessment.

Housing Restrictions

Zoning restrictions: Parolees convicted of certain sexual offenses may be restricted from residing within specified distances of schools, childcare centers, or other protected locations.

Prohibited counties or exclusion zones: Geographic exclusions may be imposed as a special condition based on victim-related or offense-related factors.

Residency approval process: Proposed housing must typically be approved by the supervising officer prior to or immediately following release. Verification may include home visits.

Co-resident background checks: Supervising officers may evaluate the criminal history of other residents in the proposed household for compatibility with supervision conditions.

Required Forms and Documentation

Official release plan: Yes. Institutional case managers may submit a structured release plan prior to release.

Interstate Compact documentation: Yes, if the parolee intends to reside outside of North Carolina.

Specific housing verification: Written verification of address and consent from primary residents is typically required.

Other state-required disclosures: Financial obligations and special conditions must be acknowledged during intake.

Unique Compliance Considerations

Drug testing frequency: Random drug testing is common. Frequency depends on supervision level and offense type.

Curfew enforcement: Curfews may be imposed as a condition and can be verified through home visits or electronic monitoring.

Electronic monitoring practices: GPS or radio-frequency monitoring may be required for certain offenses or higher supervision levels.

Travel approval procedures: Travel outside the county or state generally requires prior approval from the supervising officer.

Fees and payment structure: Monthly supervision fees may be assessed. Payment plans are typically established at intake.

Local Resources and Reentry Infrastructure

Reentry resource directories: The North Carolina Department of Adult Correction provides public reentry resource listings.

Workforce development programs: NC Works Career Centers provide employment services statewide.

Medicaid enrollment process: Parolees may apply for North Carolina Medicaid through the state Department of Health and Human Services.

Housing assistance portals: Local housing authorities and nonprofit reentry organizations may provide transitional housing or referrals.

Made in the USA
Monee, IL
04 November 2026

67381344R00036